MW01098627

Oregon 97124

Michigan

by Barbara Knox

Consultant:
Terry L. Kuseske
Teacher Consultant
Michigan Geographic Alliance
and Michigan Council for the
Social Studies

Capstone
press
Mankato, Minnesota

Capstone Press
151 Good Counsel Drive • P.O. Box 669 • Mankato, Minnesota 56002
http://www.capstone-press.com

Copyright © 2003 by Capstone Press. All rights reserved.
No part of this publication may be reproduced in whole or in part, or stored in a
retrieval system, or transmitted in any form or by any means, electronic, mechanical,
photocopying, recording, or otherwise, without written permission of the publisher.
For information regarding permission, write to Capstone Press,
151 Good Counsel Drive, P.O. Box 669, Dept. R, Mankato, Minnesota 56002.
Printed in the United States of America

Library of Congress Cataloging-in-Publication Data
Knox, Barbara.
    Michigan / by Barbara Knox.
    v. cm.—(Land of liberty)
    Contents: About Michigan—The land, climate, and wildlife—The history of
Michigan—Government and politics—Michigan's economy and resources—People
and culture.
    Includes bibliographical references (p. 61) and index.
    ISBN 0-7368-1590-2 (hardcover)
    1. Michigan—Juvenile literature. [1. Michigan.] I. Title. II. Series.
F566.3 .K59 2003
977.4—dc21   2002012068

Summary: An introduction to the geography, history, government, politics, economy,
resources, people, and culture of Michigan, including maps, charts, and a recipe.

Editorial Credits
Tom Adamson, editor; Jennifer Schonborn, series and book designer;
    Angi Gahler, illustrator; Deirdre Barton, photo researcher; Eric Kudalis,
    product planning editor

Photo Credits
Cover images: shore of Lake Superior, Visuals Unlimited/John Sohldem;
    Detroit skyline, Houserstock
Archive Photos by Getty Images, 26; Battle Creek/Calhoun County Visitor &
Convention Bureau, 38; Capstone Press/Gary Sundermeyer, 54; Corbis, 1, 34;
Corbis/Layne Kennedy, 14–15; Corbis/Bettmann, 21, 28; Corbis/Kevin Fleming,
36; Corbis/James L. Amos, 40–41; Corbis/Charles E. Rotkin, 42; Corbis/Macduff
Everton, 44; Corbis/W. Cody, 46–47; Elsa/Getty Images/NHLI, 50–51; Frederik
Meijer Gardens & Sculpture Park/Chuck Heiney Photography, 52; Houserstock,
cover (bottom); Houserstock/David G. Houser, 12, 56; Library of Congress,
24–25; One Mile Up, Inc., 55 (both); PhotoDisc, Inc., 16, 17; Stock Montage,
Inc., 18, 58; U.S. Postal Service, 59; Visuals Unlimited/John Sohldem, cover (top);
Visuals Unlimited/Mark E. Gibson, 4, 30; Visuals Unlimited/Ross Frid, 8; Visuals
Unlimited/John Meuser, 22; Visuals Unlimited/Ken Wagner, 57; Visuals
Unlimited/Robert W. Domm, 63

Artistic Elements
PhotoDisc, Inc. and Digital Stock

1 2 3 4 5 6 08 07 06 05 04 03

Table of Contents

The towers of the Mackinac Bridge rise 552 feet (168 meters) above the water.

Chapter 1

About Michigan

For many years, Michigan leaders wanted a bridge to connect the Upper and Lower Peninsulas. They knew that a bridge across the Straits of Mackinac (MAK-uh-naw) would help connect the two pieces of the state.

Michigan had to wait 120 years after statehood for its two parts to be joined. The Mackinac Bridge opened in 1957. The 5-mile (8-kilometer) bridge is sometimes called Big Mac.

Construction began in 1954. About 3,500 workers spent three years building the bridge. Almost 8,000 more workers mined rocks and crafted steel to make the parts of the bridge. The bridge has 42,000 miles (67,591 kilometers) of wire in its

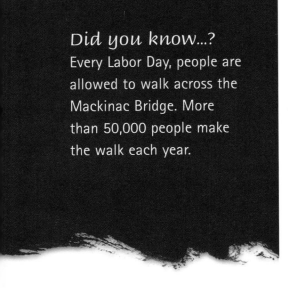

Did you know...?
Every Labor Day, people are allowed to walk across the Mackinac Bridge. More than 50,000 people make the walk each year.

cables. On June 25, 1998, Michigan celebrated the 100 millionth crossing of the Mackinac Bridge.

The Great Lakes State

Because the state is surrounded by four of the Great Lakes, Michigan is called the Great Lakes State. Lake Michigan borders the Lower Peninsula to the west. Lake Huron lies to the east, and Lake Superior is to the north. Lake Erie borders a small part of southeastern Michigan.

Michigan is the 22nd largest state. It lies in the northern United States. Detroit, the state's largest city, actually lies north of part of the province of Ontario, Canada. Ontario also borders Michigan to the north at Sault Sainte Marie. Indiana and Ohio form the land border to the south. Wisconsin borders the Upper Peninsula to the west and south.

The Lower Peninsula has big cities, factories, and farms. Most of the population lives in the Lower Peninsula. The Upper Peninsula has fewer people. It has sandy beaches and rugged, rocky land. The Upper Peninsula is often called "the U.P."

Michigan Cities

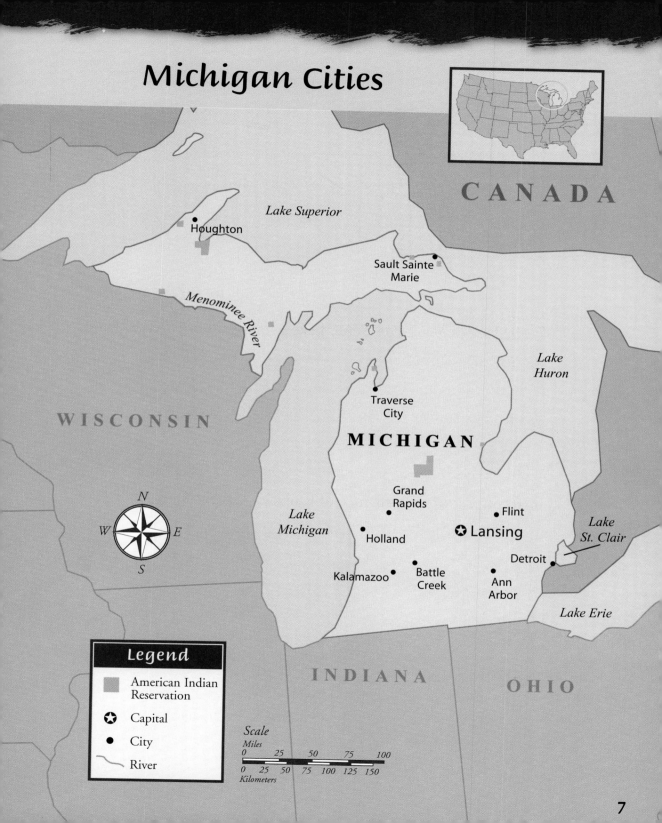

CANADA

Lake Superior

Houghton

Sault Sainte
Marie

Menominee River

WISCONSIN

Lake Huron

Traverse
City

MICHIGAN

Grand
Rapids

Flint

Lake Michigan

Holland

⭐ Lansing

Lake St. Clair

Kalamazoo

Battle
Creek

Detroit

Ann
Arbor

Lake Erie

N
W   E
S

INDIANA

OHIO

Legend

▪	American Indian Reservation
⭐	Capital
●	City
∿	River

Scale
Miles
0   25   50   75   100
0   25   50   75   100   125   150
Kilometers

The Sleeping Bear Dunes tower above
Lake Michigan.

Chapter 2

Land, Climate, and Wildlife

Michigan is almost completely surrounded by water. Michigan also has more than 11,000 lakes. The largest lake entirely within the state is Houghton Lake.

The Lower Peninsula

Sand dunes line part of the Lake Michigan shoreline. Sleeping Bear Dunes National Lakeshore is a popular tourist spot. Some sand dunes at this protected area tower 460 feet (140 meters) above Lake Michigan.

Michigan's Name

The name Michigan comes from the American Indian words "michi gama," which mean "large lake." The name might also come from the Ojibwa word "majigan," which means "clearing." The word named a clearing in the Lower Peninsula.

Farms and large cities fill the southern part of the Lower Peninsula. Detroit is in this region. Lansing, the state capital, is also in the southern part of the Lower Peninsula. Grand Rapids is another large city in the area.

Low, rolling hills cover much of the southern Lower Peninsula. The northern Lower Peninsula is a plateau that measures 1,200 to 1,500 feet (366 to 457 meters) above sea level.

Forests cover much of the northern Lower Peninsula. Hardwood trees and pines fill these forests. Many people come to see the leaves change color in fall.

Michigan's Land Features

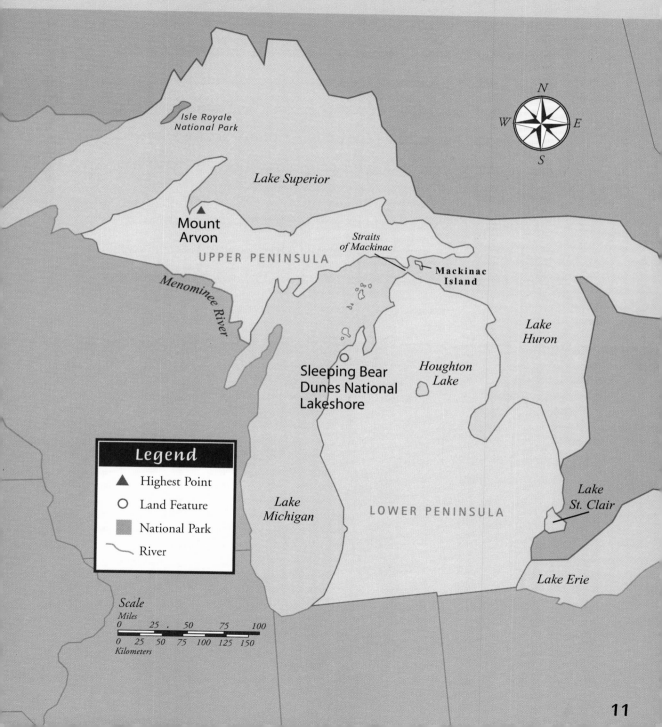

Isle Royale
National Park

Lake Superior

▲ Mount
Arvon

UPPER PENINSULA

Straits
of Mackinac

Mackinac
Island

Menominee River

Lake
Huron

Sleeping Bear
Dunes National
Lakeshore

Houghton
Lake

Lake
Michigan

LOWER PENINSULA

Lake
St. Clair

Lake Erie

Legend

▲ Highest Point
○ Land Feature
■ National Park
〜 River

Scale

Miles
0   25   .   50   75   100

0   25 50   75   100 125 150
Kilometers

The Upper Peninsula

The Upper Peninsula makes up about one-third of the state's size. The U.P. is known for its wooded mountains and waterfalls. The land is rugged in the west and swampy in the east. Mount Arvon, the state's highest point, is in the western part of the region. Michigan's copper and iron ore mines are in the U.P.

Mackinac Island sits between Michigan's two peninsulas. Cars are not allowed on the island. Most people ride bicycles. Some people also ride horses. Mackinac Island is famous for

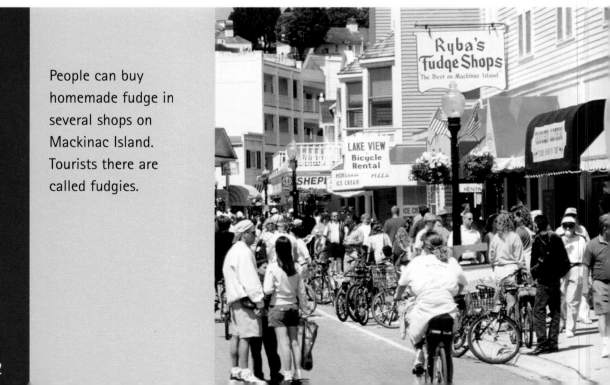

People can buy homemade fudge in several shops on Mackinac Island. Tourists there are called fudgies.

Sleeping Bear Dunes Legend

A legend explains how the Sleeping Bear Dunes formed. The story is not true, but people still enjoy it.

Long ago, a large forest fire burned in present-day Wisconsin. A mother bear and her two cubs escaped the fire by jumping into Lake Michigan. They swam for many hours, and the cubs grew tired. The mother bear reached the shore of what is now Michigan's Lower Peninsula. She climbed onto a high bluff to watch for her cubs. The cubs drowned before they could make it to shore. Two islands now mark where the two cubs drowned. A large sand dune marks the spot where the mother bear waited for her cubs.

its rocky shoreline, hiking trails, and its fudge. Several shops on the island sell homemade fudge.

Isle Royale

Isle Royale sits 22 miles (35 kilometers) from Ontario, Canada, in Lake Superior. The island is 45 miles (72 kilometers) long and almost 9 miles (14 kilometers) wide. It is the largest island in Lake Superior. Although the island is closer to Canada and Minnesota, it belongs to Michigan. The island has been a national park since 1931.

Isle Royale is one of the least visited national parks. Visitors are only allowed to go to Isle Royale between April and October. The island has no roads. Hiking trails and campgrounds draw more than 19,000 visitors every year.

Many tourists come to the island to see the wildlife. A herd of about 900 moose lives on Isle Royale. Many wolves also live there. The moose and wolves got to the island by swimming in summer or traveling over ice in winter. More

than 200 types of birds have been seen on Isle Royale. Loons and bald eagles live on the island.

Climate

On average, the Lower Peninsula is warmer than the U.P. Winters are cold across the state. But Lower Peninsula summer temperatures are warmer than those in the U.P.

The most snow in the state falls in the western U.P. An average of 160 inches (400 centimeters) of snow falls per year. Cold winter winds blow across Lake Superior. Some lake

Isle Royale National Park has 165 miles (266 kilometers) of hiking trails.

Gray wolves were once numerous in Michigan. Today, they only live on Isle Royale.

water freezes in the air and falls onto the U.P. as snow. During the winter of 1949–1950, nearly 277 inches (704 centimeters) of snow fell in Houghton.

Michigan Wildlife

Michigan's forests are home to moose, elk, black bears, and white-tailed deer. Hunting white-tailed deer is a popular

Did you know...?
The white-tailed deer is the
official state game mammal.

sport. Black bears and white-tailed
deer are the two most common
large mammals.

In the 1800s, gray wolves probably lived throughout
Michigan. But as settlers moved into the area, they pushed
the wolves out of their natural living area. Settlers also
hunted the wolves. By 1960, wolves could no longer be
found in Michigan.

A program to bring wolves back to Michigan began in
the 1970s. By the end of the 1990s, at least 174 wolves lived
on Isle Royale.

More than 400 species of birds
can be found in Michigan. Bird
watching is a popular hobby.
In the U.P., bird watchers
go to Whitefish Point Bird
Observatory. There, people
can see thousands of birds
every spring and fall when the
birds migrate through the Great
Lakes area.

Sault Sainte Marie was first established in 1668.

Chapter 3

History of Michigan

European settlers arrived in Michigan in the 1600s. At that time, nine American Indian tribes lived in the area. The Huron tribe was the largest. Other American Indian groups were the Ojibwa, Ottawa, and Potawatomi. Members of these four tribes still live in Michigan today.

The French in Michigan

French explorers began arriving in Michigan in the early 1600s. Some explorers were looking for a waterway to China and India through the Great Lakes. Others wanted to trap animals for their fur. They shipped these furs back to France and sold them. Other early French explorers wanted to teach American Indians about Christianity.

In 1688, a French priest named Jacques Marquette started the first European settlement in Michigan. Called Sault Sainte Marie, it is the third oldest city in the United States.

In 1701, a French explorer named Antoine de Lamothe Cadillac built a fort in present-day Detroit. The fort was a defense against the British, who wanted to settle the area. The fort was called Fort Pontchartrain du De Troit.

By 1751, the French had seven forts in Michigan. The British were beginning to move into the Michigan area. The French wanted to protect their fur trade from the British.

The British in Michigan

The British and French fought a series of wars from 1689 to 1763. They fought about ownership of land in North America. These wars are called the French and Indian Wars. American Indians helped the French. When the wars were over, the British took over the French forts.

Chief Pontiac

Pontiac was born around 1720 in an Ottawa village near present-day Detroit. His father was an Ottawa. His mother was Ojibwa. Those tribes worked together with the Potawatomi. Pontiac became the chief of all three tribes.

In 1763, Pontiac led an attack on the British known as Pontiac's Rebellion. American Indians took over most of the British forts in Michigan. The tribes were angry with the British over the fur trade. They were also angry because colonists were coming to live on their land. Eight of 12 planned attacks on British forts succeeded.

British troops used Michigan as a base during the Revolutionary War (1775–1783). The British encouraged American Indians to attack the American colonists. The British wanted to rule the American colonies.

In 1776, people in the 13 American colonies declared independence from Great Britain. When the colonists won the Revolutionary War in 1783, Michigan became part of the U.S. Northwest Territory. But in 1789, the British built a fort on Mackinac Island. From there, the British could control the fur trade.

The British also stayed in Fort Detroit. From there, they helped American Indians attack American settlers. U.S. soldiers finally defeated the British-backed American Indians in 1796. At that time, the United States raised the American flag over Detroit for the first time.

Today, people can visit historic Fort Mackinac. The British built the fort in 1789.

Becoming a State

Did you know...?
Stevens T. Mason became Michigan's territorial governor when he was only 22 years old.

In 1805, President Thomas Jefferson established the Michigan Territory. Few settlers wanted to go there. Michigan had thick forests. Farmers did not want to cut down trees to clear land for crops. Many farmers settled in Ohio. Because of this fact, land was cheap in Michigan.

More people began moving to Michigan after the Erie Canal was built in 1825. The canal connected the Hudson River in New York with Lake Erie. People could travel easily by boat from the East Coast to Michigan. From 1820 to 1840, the population went from 9,000 to more than 200,000.

American Indians in Michigan lost most of their land during this time. In 1836, the Treaty of Washington took land in both the Upper and Lower Peninsulas from the American Indians.

Michigan Territory and the state of Ohio disagreed about ownership of a piece of land on the border. This land now includes the city of Toledo, Ohio. Michigan claimed the land, but Ohio would not give up the land.

The governor of Michigan Territory, Stevens T. Mason, sent police to enforce Michigan's laws in the disputed area. Officers arrested many people. U.S. President Andrew Jackson removed Mason from office for this action. Mason later became the state's first governor.

In 1835, the U.S. Congress suggested a compromise. Ohio kept the land, and Michigan gained most of the Upper Peninsula. With this issue resolved, Michigan

could become a state. In 1837, Michigan became the 26th state. Detroit was the capital. In 1848, the capital was moved to Lansing because it is closer to the middle of the state.

Logging was a major business in Michigan at the end of the 1800s. Locks were built at Sault Sainte Marie to connect Lake Superior with the other Great Lakes. Locks connect rivers or lakes that are at different levels. The locks were

The Soo Locks at Sault Sainte Marie connect Lake Superior with the other Great Lakes. The locks allowed Michigan to ship goods to more parts of the country.

All of Henry Ford's Model T cars were black.

finished in 1855. They allowed lumber to be shipped to more parts of the country.

By the 1890s, the automobile industry was just beginning. In 1896, Charles King drove the first gasoline-powered car in Detroit. That same year, Henry Ford built his first car. He called it a Quadricycle.

"I will build a car for the great multitude...so low in price that no man making a good salary will be unable to own one and enjoy with his family..."

—*Henry Ford, born near Dearborn, Michigan*

Automobile Industry

The automobile business grew in the early 1900s. Ransom Olds built a factory in Lansing. He built cars called Curved Dash Olds.

William Durant had become rich selling horse-drawn wagons in Flint. In 1904, he became head of the Buick car company. In 1908, he helped organize General Motors (GM). Today, GM is one of the largest car makers.

The same year, Henry Ford built the first Model T. Mass production of the Model T made it affordable and popular. In 1914, Ford offered workers $5 a day to work in car factories. This offer brought many immigrants to Michigan.

During the Great Depression (1929–1939), unhappy autoworkers complained of poor working conditions and low pay. They formed the United Automobile Workers union in 1935. In 1936, workers in Flint held a sit-down strike. They stayed in the factory and refused to work or leave.

After more than one month, GM agreed to allow the workers to form a labor union. Other car companies allowed workers to form unions. Workers could now work together to demand higher pay and better working conditions. The strike made Michigan a strong union state. The Flint strike also strengthened labor unions in the rest of the country.

Workers at a car factory in Flint staged a sit-down strike in 1936. They refused to work until they got better pay and better working conditions.

Changes and Growth

In 1957, the Mackinac Bridge opened. The bridge connected the U.P. with the Lower Peninsula. By the end of the 1990s, more than 2 million vehicles crossed the bridge every year.

During the 1960s and 1970s, African Americans struggled for equal rights in Michigan and across the country. In 1963, Martin Luther King Jr. led a civil rights march in Detroit. He gave his "I Have a Dream" speech for the first time. Struggles between African Americans and whites took place during the 1960s. Race riots destroyed parts of Detroit. African Americans were angry about unfair and unequal treatment.

In the 1970s and 1980s, fuel costs went up, making cars cost more to drive. Car companies sold fewer cars. Many people moved out of the state.

Even though the car industry is still important today, many people are now working in new businesses. Kalamazoo and Ann Arbor are important centers for medical research and the production of medicines.

The governor works in the capitol building, located in Lansing.

Chapter 4

Government and Politics

Like the United States, Michigan has three branches of government. The executive, legislative, and judicial branches work together to make and enforce laws.

Three Branches of Government

The governor's main job is to make sure people follow Michigan's laws. The legislature sends bills to the governor to be signed into law. The governor makes a plan for spending the state's money. The governor is elected to a four-year term.

"Truth is the glue that holds government together."
—Gerald R. Ford, 38th president of the United States

Michigan has a full-time legislature. Lawmakers work year-round. They make new laws for Michigan. In a two-year period, the Michigan legislature will consider about 4,000 bills. They will pass 600 to 800 bills into law.

The Michigan legislature includes the senate and the house of representatives. Each state representative is elected to a two-year term. Each state senator serves a four-year term. Each senator represents more than 200,000 people from his or her district.

Hundreds of different courts make up the Michigan judicial branch. This branch interprets the state's laws. The state supreme court is the highest court. It has the final say in any court case in the state.

Like all other states, Michigan sends two senators to the U.S. Senate. Michigan also has 15 representatives in the U.S. House of Representatives. The state lost one representative after the 2000 census. Michigan's population did not grow as fast as some western and southern states' populations did. Some of these states added representatives as a result.

Michigan's Government

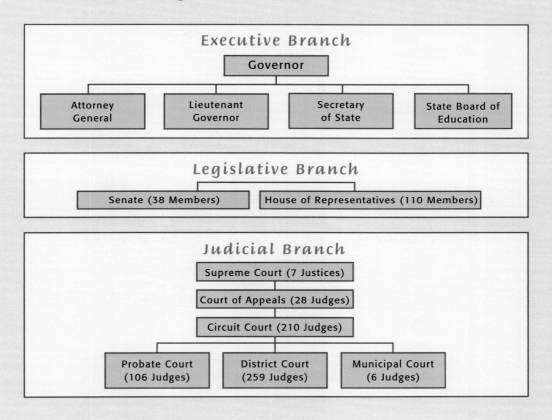

Executive Branch

Governor

- Attorney General
- Lieutenant Governor
- Secretary of State
- State Board of Education

Legislative Branch

- Senate (38 Members)
- House of Representatives (110 Members)

Judicial Branch

- Supreme Court (7 Justices)
- Court of Appeals (28 Judges)
- Circuit Court (210 Judges)
- Probate Court (106 Judges)
- District Court (259 Judges)
- Municipal Court (6 Judges)

Michigan Politics

Both major political parties, the Democrats and Republicans, are active in Michigan. Republicans were mostly in power from 1855 to 1964. Michigan is known as the birthplace of the Republican Party.

After World War II (1939–1945), the Democratic Party became stronger in Michigan. G. Mennen Williams served as governor from 1949 to 1960. Williams helped strengthen the Democratic Party in the state.

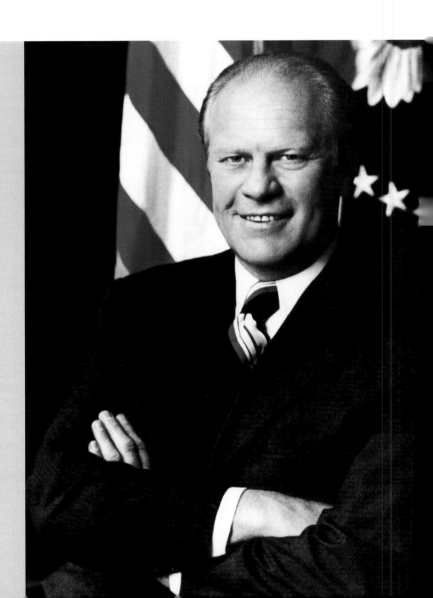

Gerald R. Ford served as president of the United States from 1974 to 1977.

Did you know...?
Gerald Ford is the only
person to serve as both vice
president and president
without having been elected
to either office.

Republican Gerald R. Ford is the most famous politician from Michigan. He was a member of the U.S. House of Representatives from 1948 to 1973. In 1973, Vice President Spiro Agnew resigned. President Richard Nixon named Ford to take Agnew's place. Just eight months later, President Nixon resigned. Ford then became president. He lost the 1976 election to Jimmy Carter. The Gerald R. Ford Museum in Grand Rapids has many exhibits about Ford's presidency.

Michigan is usually a key state in presidential elections. Because of Michigan's manufacturing industry, it is a strong labor union state. Unions are usually very involved in presidential elections. Michigan is also considered to be representative of the United States as a whole. The state is near the middle of the country, and the population is diverse. Candidates for president usually spend much time campaigning in Michigan.

The automobile industry is still an important part of Michigan's economy.

Chapter 5

West Union School
23870 NW West Union Road
Hillsboro, Oregon 97124

Economy and Resources

Car manufacturing is still an important industry in Michigan. But people in many Michigan cities are working in new types of businesses.

Manufacturing

Michigan's automobile industry was a big part of the American Industrial Revolution in the early 1900s. At that time, people learned to make things faster and cheaper in factories. This process was called mass production. Many mass production methods were invented in Michigan for building cars.

Each June, Battle Creek has the Cereal City Festival, which features the world's longest breakfast table.

Michigan became a leader in the car industry for many reasons. Many wealthy Michigan business owners made money in mining and logging. They had the money for new businesses. Michigan had been a center for buggy manufacturing. Cars began to replace buggies in the early

"When I was working in the [car] factory, I used to write during breaks because it took me away from being in the factory."
—Christopher Curtis, children's book author, born in Flint, Michigan

1900s. Workers switched from making buggies to making cars. Dearborn, Flint, Detroit, Lansing, and Pontiac have all been key car manufacturing cities.

Colleges are now helping Michigan's businesses depend less on building cars. Companies in Michigan now produce chemicals and new medicines. People do medical research at the state's colleges.

Other cities in Michigan also make other products. Midland has large chemical plants. Saginaw, Grand Rapids, Bay City, and Muskegon are other major industrial cities. Kalamazoo was once known for its paper manufacturing plants. Many paper plants have closed. Programs at Western Michigan University are trying to help keep these plants open.

Battle Creek produces more breakfast cereal than any other city in the world. In the 1890s, the Kellogg brothers experimented with grains. They mashed and rolled wheat and cooked the dough as flakes. This experiment led to cornflakes, which is still a popular breakfast cereal today.

Agriculture

Southern Michigan enjoys a long growing season. Moisture from Lake Michigan protects the land along the coast from frost. Farmers there can plant earlier in spring and harvest later in fall than in colder parts of the state. Grain and corn farmers take advantage of this long growing season in the southern part of the Lower Peninsula.

Orchards can be found along the Lake Michigan shoreline. Cherries, plums, peaches, and grapes are the main fruit crops. Michigan grapes are made into juice and wine.

Michigan grows more tart cherries than any other state. Every year, the state produces between 200 million and 250 million pounds (91 million and 113 million kilograms) of tart cherries. It also produces about 50 million pounds (23 million kilograms) of sweet cherries. Both types of cherries are usually harvested around the third week of July. The state celebrates its cherries every year in July at the National Cherry Festival in Traverse City.

An average tart cherry tree holds about 7,000 cherries. One tree holds enough cherries for 28 cherry pies. These

Traverse City is the center for cherry production in Michigan.

cherries are almost never sold fresh. They are usually canned or frozen. Tart cherries are used in pie fillings, jams and jellies, pastries, juices, and many other products.

Tourism

Michigan's scenery and events draw many tourists to the state. Tourists spend money at restaurants, stores, and hotels. People visit beaches or the rocky shoreline. They hike in the forests and mountains. Tourists also go to festivals and museums.

Iron ore mines operate in the Upper Peninsula.

High-Speed Internet

In 2002, Governor John Engler signed three bills to make high-speed Internet connections available to everyone in the state. The bills are called the MI HiSpeed Internet plan. Experts believe the bills will help create 500,000 new jobs for Michigan. The new Internet plan could bring as much as $440 billion to Michigan during the next 10 years.

Natural Resources

From 1845 to 1877, Michigan produced more copper than any other part of North America. Most of the copper is now gone. Michigan's last copper mine closed in 1995. Today, Michigan mining focuses on iron ore.

Michigan's forests are another important resource. Tourism and the furniture and paper industries all depend on Michigan's forests.

The Ottawa Homecoming Powwow takes place every August in Harbor Springs. This town was once the capital of the Ottawa Nation. The powwow includes dance contests.

People and Culture

Michigan is home to more than 120 ethnic groups. In the 1800s, Michigan was a popular place for immigrants. They moved to Michigan because of the fresh water, forests, minerals, and farmland.

American Indians

European settlers came to Michigan in the 1600s. At that time, several thousand American Indians lived in the area. Today, Michigan has one of the 10 largest American Indian populations in the United States. Three main tribes live in

Detroit

More than 1 million people live in Detroit. It is the home to the "Big Three" car companies in the United States. General Motors, Ford, and DaimlerChrysler have their main offices in or near Detroit. Because of its long history with cars, Detroit got the nickname "Motor City," sometimes shortened to "Motown."

Detroit stretches along the Detroit River. It sits between Lake Erie and Lake St. Clair. People can drive through the Detroit-Windsor Tunnel to reach Canada.

Most of Detroit's population is African American. According to the 2000 census, nearly 82 percent of Detroit's people are African American.

Michigan. The Ojibwa, Ottawa, and Potawatomi tribes are called the "People of the Three Fires." Michigan Indians hold a wide variety of jobs. Many American Indians continue to do traditional jobs, such as fishing and harvesting rice.

Michigan Indians are citizens of the United States and of their tribe. They have dual citizenship. Many of them keep their tribal customs. Since the 1990s, tribes have built

gambling casinos. Fishing and hunting rights are also important issues for many American Indians.

European Heritage

Most people in Michigan have European backgrounds. More than 1.5 million Michigan citizens are Polish. Many Poles moved to Michigan in the early 1900s when Henry Ford was offering jobs that paid $5 a day.

About 120,000 Dutch people settled around Grand Rapids and Holland in the mid-1800s. Tulips are a symbol of Dutch heritage. Today, tulip festivals are still popular with tourists. The Holland Tulip Time Festival is considered to be one of the top events in the United States.

More than 1 million Michiganians have German ancestors. Many Germans settled in Michigan in the 1800s. Michigan leaders hired promoters to find new people to settle in the state. Germans were thought to be hardworking, religious

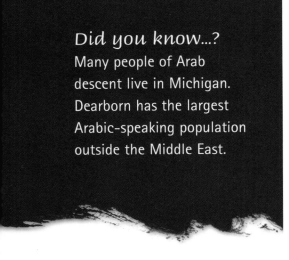

Did you know...?
Many people of Arab descent live in Michigan. Dearborn has the largest Arabic-speaking population outside the Middle East.

people. The promoters went to Germany to convince people to move to Michigan.

In the U.P., the largest ethnic group comes from Finland. While many Finns moved to Michigan to work as lumberjacks or miners, most became farmers. In the 1800s, Finns in this area were the largest group of Finns in the United States. They started their own college, Suomi College, in 1896. The school is now called Finlandia University.

African Americans

Michigan was an important part of the Underground Railroad in the 1800s. This system of safe houses helped slaves escape the South and start new lives in other places. Many African Americans chose to settle in Michigan. Nathan Thomas, from the town of Schoolcraft, helped more than 1,000 slaves escape to freedom. The Second Baptist Church in Detroit was also a stop on the Underground Railroad. Close to the Canadian border, this site helped slaves escape to Canada.

Michigan's Ethnic Backgrounds

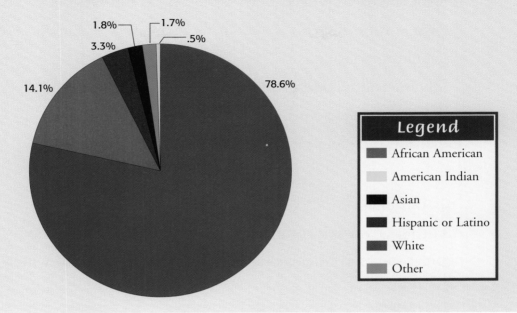

1.8% 1.7%
3.3% .5%
14.1%
78.6%

Legend
- African American
- American Indian
- Asian
- Hispanic or Latino
- White
- Other

In the 1900s, more immigrants and more southerners headed for Michigan to work in car factories. African Americans from the South also moved to Michigan to work in fruit orchards. The African American population soared to 200,000 by the mid-1900s. In 2000, African Americans made up more than 14 percent of Michigan's population.

New Immigrants

Hispanics are the fastest-growing ethnic group in Michigan. In the early 2000s, Hispanics made up the largest group of foreign language speakers in the state. An area in Detroit known as Mexicantown is famous for its many Mexican restaurants and shops.

By the end of 1999, Asians made up about 26 percent of new immigrants to Michigan. People from China, Korea, India, and the Philippines have moved to Michigan.

Sports

All pro sports have teams in Michigan. One of the most popular sports in Michigan is hockey. Hockey's popularity in

Canada spreads into Michigan. Fans have cheered for the Detroit Red Wings since 1926. People sometimes call Detroit Hockeytown. The Red Wings won the Stanley Cup in 1997, 1998, and again in 2002.

In basketball, the Detroit Pistons won NBA Championships in 1989 and 1990. In women's pro basketball, the Detroit Shock are the WNBA team.

The Detroit Tigers have been Michigan's pro baseball team since 1901. Ty Cobb was the team's most famous player. The Tigers last won a World Series in 1984. Today, minor league

The Detroit Red Wings defeated the Carolina Hurricanes to win the Stanley Cup in 2002.

baseball is becoming more popular. People in Kalamazoo, Grand Rapids, Flint, Battle Creek, and Lansing can watch semi-pro baseball at lower prices than major league games.

Football has always been popular in Michigan. The University of Michigan Wolverines have loyal fans nationwide. Michigan State University also has a strong football program. The Lions have been Detroit's pro football team since 1934.

The Frederik Meijer Gardens and Sculpture Park in Grand Rapids has many outdoor sculptures. This sculpture is called Aria.

The Arts

The large cities in the Lower Peninsula have many art museums and specialty museums. The Henry Ford Museum in Dearborn offers information and exhibits on the history of the car in the United States. The Detroit Institute of Arts is thought to be one of the great art museums of the world. At the Frederik Meijer Gardens and Sculpture Park in Grand Rapids, visitors can see sculptures by famous artists.

In the U.P., the Great Lakes Shipwreck Museum has a collection of information about many famous wrecks. The U.S. National Ski Hall of Fame is located in the U.P.

Michigan was once known only for car factories and other manufacturing. Today, the people of Michigan are expanding into other technological businesses. While car factories are still important, higher education and tourism are new opportunities for Michigan.

Did you know...?
Michigan was the first state in the country to establish public libraries through its constitution. It was also the first state to guarantee every child the right to a tax-paid high school education.

Recipe: Cherry S'mores

Michigan grows more tart cherries than any other state in the country. This recipe is a quick and easy way to have dried tart cherries in a snack.

Ingredients

½ cup (120 mL) marshmallow creme
½ cup (120 mL) dried tart cherries
¼ cup (60 mL) semisweet chocolate chips
12 graham cracker squares

Equipment

dry-ingredient measuring cups
medium bowl
wooden spoon
microwave-safe plate
table spoon
hot pad

What You Do

1. Put marshmallow creme, cherries, and chocolate chips in a medium bowl. Mix with a wooden spoon.

2. Place six of the graham crackers on a microwave-safe plate. Place a heaping spoonful of marshmallow mixture on each cracker. Top with remaining crackers.

3. Microwave uncovered on High (100 percent power) for 10 seconds, or until marshmallow mixture is soft and warm. Carefully remove plate from the microwave and set on a hot pad. Let the s'mores cool slightly before eating them.

Makes 6 cherry s'mores

Michigan's Flag and Seal

Michigan's Flag

Michigan's flag is a field of blue with the state seal in the center. The flag once showed Michigan's first governor, Stevens T. Mason, on one side. On the other side was the state coat of arms. In 1865, the flag was changed to show the U.S. coat of arms on one side and the Michigan coat of arms on the other. The current flag was adopted in 1911.

Michigan's State Seal

Michigan's state seal was approved in 1911. The bald eagle on the top of the seal stands for the United States. The elk on the left and the moose on the right represent Michigan. The state motto appears on the seal, "Si Quaeris Peninsulam Amoenam Circumspice." These Latin words mean, "If you seek a pleasant peninsula, look about you."

Almanac

Nickname: Great Lakes State

Population: 9,938,444 (U.S. Census 2000)
Population rank: 8th

Capital: Lansing

Largest cities: Detroit, Grand Rapids, Flint, Lansing, Ann Arbor

Agricultural products: Tart cherries, sweet cherries, corn, soybeans, wheat, oats, apples, plums, peaches

Average summer temperature: 66 degrees Fahrenheit (19 degrees Celsius)

Average winter temperature: 22 degrees Fahrenheit (minus 6 degrees Celsius)

Average annual precipitation: 31 inches (79 centimeters)

Area: 58,216 square miles (150,779 square kilometers)
Size rank: 22nd

Highest point: Mount Arvon, 1,980 feet (604 meters) above sea level

Lowest point: Lake Erie, 572 feet (174 meters) above sea level

Tart cherries

Economy

Natural resources:
Oil, natural gas,
iron ore, salt, forests,
the Great Lakes

Types of industry:
Cars, machinery,
cereal, food processing,
medicines, chemicals,
paper

Symbols

Bird: Robin

Fish: Brook trout

Flower: Apple blossom

Symbols

Game mammal:
White-tailed deer

Reptile: Painted turtle

Song: "Michigan, My
Michigan" by Douglas
M. Malloch

Stone: Petoskey stone

Tree: White pine

Government

First governor:
Stevens T. Mason

Statehood: January 26,
1837 (26th state)

U.S. Representatives: 15

U.S. Senators: 2

U.S. electoral votes: 17

Counties: 83

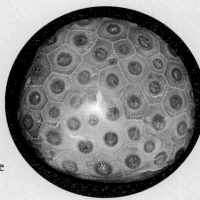

Petoskey stone

Timeline

State History

1600s
French explorers and fur traders first meet the native peoples of what is now Michigan.

1668
Father Jacques Marquette establishes the first mission at Sault Sainte Marie.

1701
Antoine de Lamothe Cadillac builds a fort in present-day Detroit.

1763
Pontiac and his soldiers capture eight of 12 British forts in Michigan.

1837
On January 26, Michigan becomes the 26th state.

1800s
Abolitionists in Michigan help slaves escape to Canada on the Underground Railroad.

U.S. History

1620
Pilgrims establish a colony in the New World.

1763
Great Britain wins the French and Indian Wars.

1775–1783
American colonists and the British fight the Revolutionary War.

1861–1865
The Union and the Confederacy fight the Civil War.

1908
The first Model T
Ford is built.

1936
Workers at a
Flint car factory
stage a sit-down
strike.

1914
Henry Ford
offers workers
$5 a day to
work in his car
factories.

1974
Gerald R. Ford
becomes the 38th
president when
Richard Nixon resigns.

2002
The MI HiSpeed
Internet plan is
adopted.

1957
The Mackinac
Bridge opens.

1929–1939
Many Americans
lose jobs during the
Great Depression.

2001
On September 11,
terrorists attack the
World Trade Center
and the Pentagon.

1964
U.S. Congress
passes the Civil
Rights Act, which
makes any form
of discrimination
illegal.

1914–1918
World War I is
fought; the
United States
enters the war
in 1917.

1939–1945
World War II
is fought; the
United States
enters the war
in 1941.

Words to Know

campaign (kam-PAYN)—to try to gain support from people in order to win an election

canal (kuh-NAL)—a channel that people dig across land; the Erie Canal connects the Hudson River and Lake Erie so that ships can travel between them.

immigrant (IM-uh-gruhnt)—a person who comes from one country to live in another country

locks (LOKS)—a part of a canal where boats are raised or lowered to different water levels

mammal (MAM-uhl)—a warm-blooded animal with a backbone

mass production (MASS pruh-DUHK-shuhn)—a system of making products on an assembly line; mass production made cars affordable.

peninsula (puh-NIN-suh-luh)—a piece of land that is surrounded by water on three sides; Michigan is made up of two peninsulas.

plateau (pla-TOH)—an area of high, flat land

union (YOON-yuhn)—an organized group of workers set up to help improve working conditions, pay, and benefits

To Learn More

Barenblat, Rachel. *Michigan, the Wolverine State*. World Almanac Library of the States. Milwaukee: World Almanac Library, 2002.

Burgan, Michael. *Henry Ford*. Trailblazers of the Modern World. Milwaukee: World Almanac Library, 2002.

Hintz, Martin. *Michigan*. America the Beautiful. New York: Children's Press, 1998.

Sirvaitis, Karen. *Michigan*. Hello U.S.A. Minneapolis: Lerner, 2002.

Internet Sites

Track down many sites about Michigan.
Visit the FACT HOUND at *http://www.facthound.com*

IT IS EASY! IT IS FUN!
1) Go to *http://www.facthound.com*
2) Type in: 0736815902
3) Click on "FETCH IT" and FACT HOUND will find several links hand-picked by our editors.

Relax and let our pal FACT HOUND do the research for you!

Places to Write and Visit

Henry Ford Museum and Greenfield Village
20900 Oakwood Boulevard
Dearborn, MI 48124-4088

Kellogg's Cereal City USA
171 West Michigan Avenue
Battle Creek, MI 49017

Mackinaw Area Tourist Bureau
10300 South U.S. 23
P.O. Box 160
Mackinaw City, MI 49701

Michigan Historical Center
702 West Kalamazoo Street
Lansing, MI 48909-8240

The Office of the Governor
P.O. Box 30013
Lansing, MI 48909

Sleeping Bear Dunes National Lakeshore
9922 Front Street
Empire, MI 49630-9797

Wagner Falls is located in the
Upper Peninsula of Michigan.

Index

T 57127

West Union School
23870 NW West Union Road
Hillsboro, Oregon 97124